ABOUT THE ONE EARTH BOOKS

During its nearly one hundred years of educating the public about environmental issues, the National Audubon Society has rarely achieved anything as important as reaching out to the world's young people, the voices of tomorrow. For Audubon and its 600,000 members, nothing is so crucial as ensuring that those voices speak in the future on behalf of wildlife.

Audubon reaches out to people in many ways—through its nationwide system of wildlife sanctuaries, through research vital to helping set the nation's environmental policy, through lobbying for sound conservation laws, through television documentaries and fact-based dramatic films, through *Audubon* magazine and computer software, and through ecology workshops for adults and Audubon Adventures clubs in school classrooms. Each of these is critical to reaching a large audience. And now, with the Audubon One Earth books, the environmental community can speak to the youngest minds in our citizenry.

Audubon is proud to publish One Earth in cooperation with Bantam Books. In addition to bringing new information and experiences to young readers, these books will instill in them a fundamental concern for the environment and its decline at the hands of humanity. They will also, it is hoped, stimulate an undying interest in the natural world that will empower young people, as they mature, to protect the world's natural wonders for themselves and for future generations.

We at Audubon hope you will enjoy the One Earth books and that you will find in them an inspiration for joining our earth-saving mission. Young people are the hope for our future.

Christopher N. Palmer
Executive Editor
President, National Audubon
Society Productions

ONE EARTH

WHERE ARE MY PRAIRIE DOGS AND BLACK-FOOTED FERRETS?

RON HIRSCHI

Photographs by ERWIN and PEGGY BAUER and others

National
Audubon
Society

BANTAM BOOKS · NEW YORK · TORONTO · LONDON · SYDNEY · AUCKLAND

For Hope

If you would like to receive more
information about the National Audubon Society write to:

National Audubon Society, Membership Department,
950 Third Avenue, New York, NY 10022

WHERE ARE MY PRAIRIE DOGS AND BLACK-FOOTED FERRETS?
A Bantam Book / October 1992

Executive Editor: Christopher N. Palmer

Library of Congress Cataloging in Publication Data

Hirschi, Ron.
    Where are my prairie dogs and black-footed ferrets? / by Ron Hirschi; photographs by Erwin and Peggy Bauer.
        p.   cm. — (One earth)
    "A National Audubon Society book."
    Summary: Describes the lifestyle and habitat of the prairie dog and black-footed ferret, how the destruction of the grasslands
threatens their survival, and what you can do to save the animals.
    ISBN 0-553-07802-X. — ISBN 0-553-35471-X (pbk.)
    1. Prairie fauna—Juvenile literature.   2. Prairie fauna—United States—Juvenile literature.   3. Prairie dogs—Juvenile
literature.   4. Black-footed ferret—Juvenile literature.   5. Endangered species—United States—Juvenile literature.   [1. Prairie
dogs.   2. Black footed ferret.   3. Ferret.   4. Rare animals.   5. Wildlife conservation.]   I. Bauer, Erwin A., ill.   II. Bauer,
Peggy, ill.   III. Title.   IV. Series: Hirschi, Ron. One earth.
QL115.3.H57   1992
333.95'9—dc20   91-13406   CIP   AC

Published simultaneously in the United States and Canada

Bantam Books are published by Bantam Books, a division of Bantam Doubleday Dell Publishing Group, Inc. Its trademark,
consisting of the words "Bantam Books" and the portrayal of a rooster, is Registered in U.S. Patent and Trademark Office and in
other countries. Marca Registrada. Bantam Books, 666 Fifth Avenue, New York, New York 10103.

PRINTED IN THE UNITED STATES OF AMERICA

0 9 8 7 6 5 4 3 2 1

INTRODUCTION

Green grass surrounds us in yards, parks, and playgrounds. Farmers nurture hay crops and ranchers raise cattle in pastures where wild grasslands once grew. What about the wide-open prairies that once stretched freely across the western and central states? Where have they all gone? What is the fate of prairie wildlife such as prairie dogs and the rarest mammal in North America, the black-footed ferret?

Join us as we travel from the places where many of us live in comfort to the grasslands of the western United States where prairie dogs and ferrets need our help to save their vanishing homes.

Walk with me past fields where you play soccer or run with your pup.

Watch as the robins take a bath in the sprinkler or hunt for fat worms.

See the goldfinch search all the edges where the lawn is never mowed. Here they might find their favorite thistle seeds.

Then follow a garter snake as it slithers through the thick green grass.

Follow to where the wild rose grows, to where birds sing from perches on sunflower stems and cottonwood trees.

You might see a rabbit nibbling some clover.
But where are my prairie dogs? They once lived
here, too.

Farther from the city, where farm fiel

etch beyond distant hills . . .

wild geese nibble tender sprouts and

pheasants hide in rows of sweet corn.

Red foxes and coyotes sneak, then leap to catch a mouse for breakfast in hay fields that grow up to your ears.

But where are the prairie dogs?
Have you heard their barking call?

Far from the biggest cities, between the western mountains and the Great Plains, golden eagles still soar above shortgrass prairie rarely touched by human hands.

Here you might find prairie dogs barking in their prairie dog towns. You might find their tunnels, dug deep underground.

Watch burrowing owls search these tunnels for a nest of their own.

Watch falcons swoop in fast flight. And sniff
the fresh air for the scent of sweet sage.

Here in the land of the badger, where buffalo
grass grows silvery green, you can hear the little
dogs bark. You can see a prairie dog hug and a
prairie dog kiss.

In the time when buffalo roamed in great, thundering herds, prairie dog towns grew to prairie dog cities of millions and more.

Then came people with poison, guns, and sharp plows . . . then prairie grassland turned into farms, dust, and ranches for cows.

Where pronghorns ran free as the wind, the once endless prairie grew quiet. Quiet and still.

Now, where can you hear a prairie dog bark and a prairie dog yip? And where can the black-footed ferret hunt its favorite, prairie dog meal?

Ferrets need prairie dogs like you need food to eat and water to drink.

Majestic eagles can hunt mice or ground squirrels.

Meadowlarks can sing and hunt on farms planted with crops. And robins can hunt worms on grass grown as a lawn.

LuRay Parker/Wyoming Game & Fish Department

But without wild prairie grasslands, prairie dogs
will soon vanish and their sleek masked hunters,
the ferrets, will all disappear.

Not long ago, out in Wyoming, beneath the wide prairie sky, a black-footed ferret was discovered, then just a few more.

Rare as any animal is rare, the last few ferrets need homes in vast prairie dog towns.

We must save the grasslands, the last prairie dog towns, and black-footed ferrets, too. We must keep the balance of nature. It is all up to you.

AFTERWORD

For young readers, parents, teachers,
big brothers, and big sisters:

Delicate balances among plants, bison, prairie dogs, black-footed ferrets, and other wildlife once determined the composition of grasslands east of the Rocky Mountains. Silver-green buffalo grass thrived through droughts for centuries before the coming of the plow. But severe overgrazing by cattle, decimation of the buffalo herds, and humanity's direct attempts to eliminate prairie dogs quickly altered much of the shortgrass prairie.

Ranchers shot and poisoned prairie dogs and even introduced deadly bubonic plague to try to drive them to extinction. Even today, people celebrate shooting prairie dogs as part of a Colorado community event. As a result of prairie dog declines, their predators—black-footed ferrets—are in even greater danger. At present fewer than 200 black-footed ferrets are known to exist, all in captivity. To survive, some of those in captivity must be released into the wild, in several locations, to protect the entire population from being subject to diseases or threats from humans in any one location.

In some states, the law actually requires that prairie dogs be killed. In others, many ranchers have voluntarily agreed to help prairie dogs and ferrets live together on private land. On Navajo land, prairie dogs have survived together with people for centuries. Their example offers the greatest hope for protection of natural balances including grasslands, prairie dogs, and the endangered black-footed ferrets.

We urge you and your young reader to visit the shortgrass prairies of the West, searching for prairie dog towns and the rare black-footed ferret. Once you have seen them, you may discover new ways to help save their special home.

ACTIVITIES

Things you can do to help save prairie dogs, black-footed ferrets, and other wildlife of prairies and grasslands:

• Plant a wild grassland "prairie" of your own. Purchase native grass seed or sod from your local nursery or collect seeds by running through a meadow while wearing fuzzy socks. Come back home and pluck the seeds from your sock seed collectors, then sprinkle them in your own "prairie" garden.

• Encourage others to grow wildflower gardens instead of lawns. Select plants native to your backyard. (Help with this can be found in the library and from your state natural resource agency responsible for protecting rare and endangered plants.)

• Allow wild flowers to grow where mowing isn't necessary.

- Keep your own set of nature notes on the plants and animals that return to these grassy areas.

- As a school project, create a native prairie or grassland habitat area on your school grounds.

- Place sunflower-seed bird feeders in your backyard and at school, allowing the seeds that fall to the ground to sprout and grow into a sunflower garden.

- As a school project, adopt prairie dogs and black-footed ferrets. Get to know more about their needs and write letters to congressional representatives and the U.S. secretary of the interior, urging them to support federal funding for black-footed ferret captive breeding and reintroduction programs.

- Visit the shortgrass prairies of the West with family, friends, and classmates . . . perhaps together, you can discover new ways to save the grasslands, prairie dog towns, and black-footed ferrets, too.

ABOUT THE AUTHOR

Ron Hirschi is a renowned environmentalist who worked as a habitat biologist before turning full time to writing and working with children. He now visits children in classrooms and communities nationwide, inspiring their curiosity and helping them to see that there are many things they can do in their own backyards to make our earth a better place.

Ron has written twenty books for children, including the acclaimed *Winter* and *Spring* books and the recently published Discover My World series.

ABOUT THE PHOTOGRAPHERS

Erwin and Peggy Bauer and the other contributors are among the world's most highly regarded wildlife photographers. Together the Bauers have published over twenty-five books and countless articles about their worldwide photographic expeditions.

The prairie dogs featured in this book were photographed at Devils Tower National Monument (Wyoming) and in Wind Cave National Park (South Dakota). The black-footed ferrets were photographed in Meeteetse, Wyoming.